ALBERT EINSTEIN

Chris Oxlade

W
FRANKLIN WATTS
LONDON•SYDNEY

Illustrations Ian Thompson
Designer Thomas Keenes
Editor Constance Novis
Art Director Jonathan Hair
Editor-in-Chief John C. Miles
Picture Research Susan Mennell

Consultant Eileen Yeo
Professor of Social and Cultural
History, University of Strathclyde

First published in 2003
by Franklin Watts
96 Leonard Street
London
EC2A 4XD

Franklin Watts Australia
45-51 Huntley Street
Alexandria
NSW 2015

ISBN 0 7496 4646 2

A CIP catalogue record
for this book is available
from the British Library.

Printed in Hong Kong/China

Picture credits
Front cover: main photograph AKG
London; background Hulton Archive
Back cover: AKG London

AKG London pp. 2, 3, 5, 7,14, 16-17,
21 top, 21 bottom, 22, 25, 26, 29, 37
(Erich Lessing), 41, 44 (Sotheby's), 50,
53, 56-57, 58, 63, 69, 71, 73, 75, 76,
77, 80-81(Dieter E. Hoppe), 83, 84,
87, 92-93, 97
Albert Einstein Archives, Jerusalem
pp. 8, 54
Mary Evans Picture Library pp. 31, 32,
43, 66
Hulton Archive 47, 88-89
Popperfoto pp. 18 (Reuters), 78-79,
94, 105
SPL pp. 38l, 38r, 48-49 (Alex Bartel),
64 (Dr. Fred Espenak), 99 (Space
Telescope Science Institute/NASA),
101 (Patrice Loiez, Cern), 102 (James
King-Holmes)
Stadtarchiv, Ulm pp.10-11

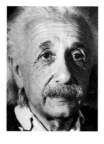

Albert Einstein 1879–1955

Contents

Introduction

Albert Einstein (1879–1955) was probably the most famous scientist who ever lived. His theories challenged the way scientists thought about the nature of matter and the universe.

To this day, Einstein remains one of the most written about scientists ever, and his name is used as another word for genius.

He was born in Germany and went to school there, later attending college in Zürich, Switzerland. Surprisingly, Einstein was not a child genius or a high-flier at school or college. As a young man he earned his living as a humble clerk in the Swiss patent office in Bern. But all the time he was developing his own theories on physics, and he published several of them in 1905. This work gained him recognition in the scientific community, and from 1909 he worked as a university lecturer and researcher, teaching students and developing more ideas. He became world-famous when his theory of general relativity was shown to be true in 1919.

In 1933 Einstein decided to take up residence in the USA because he was a Jew and it was no longer safe for him to remain in Berlin. The persecution of Jews, a form of racism known as anti-Semitism, was on the rise in Germany, where such persecution was soon to become enshrined in law. He lived in the USA for the last 22 years of his life. Over the years he changed nationality several times, from German to Swiss, back to German and then to American. He married twice and had three children.

Einstein was a theoretical physicist. His theories predicted things that seemed incredible at the time and many scientists could not understand some of his ideas. However, most of Einstein's predictions have turned out to be true. His most famous work involved his theories of relativity. These provided new and revolutionary ways of thinking about space, time and gravity and included the famous equation $E=mc^2$.

Einstein was also a pacifist and a humanist. He campaigned for peace and disarmament, and supported Zionism, the movement for a homeland for the Jews.

▲ *A portrait photograph of Einstein taken around 1954.*

Einstein's childhood

Albert Einstein was born on 14 March 1879 in Ulm in southern Germany. He was a large baby, with an unusually shaped head.

Albert's parents, Pauline and Hermann, were shocked by his appearance. But by the time he was a few months old, he looked like any normal child, just as their doctor had said he would.

Hermann Einstein was an electrical engineer. He ran his own electrochemical business with his brother, Jakob, whose family shared the Einsteins' apartment. Pauline Koch Einstein came from a wealthy family. Both Hermann and Pauline were Jews, but they did not practise Jewish religious customs. Albert had one sister, called Maja. She was two and a half years younger than he was.

No genius

Albert was not a child genius. In his first few years, there was no sign that he would become one of the greatest minds of all time. In fact, Albert took longer than other children to start talking. His parents were concerned that he had learning difficulties, but it turned out that he was just naturally quiet. Later in life, Einstein laughed about this, saying that he did not think it was worth speaking until he could use proper sentences.

Electrical industries

The late nineteenth century was a time of industrial expansion in Europe. Engineers had worked out how to generate and control electricity on a large scale, and industries were just beginning to make use of it. The electrical industry itself was very important to the economy of Germany. However, powerful companies such as Siemens made life difficult for small businesses like the Einsteins'.

▶ *A family photograph of Albert Einstein at the age of six with his four-year-old sister, Maja.*

▶ Albert's parents, Hermann and Pauline Einstein.

A move to Munich

When Albert was born the family business was not making any money. Ulm was a small city, with only a few industries that would buy their products. Jakob suggested that they move to Munich, a booming industrial city where there would be more customers. So in 1881 both families moved to a house in Munich. Hermann and Jakob set up a factory where they made dynamos and arc lights. Sadly, business was no better.

Before Albert was old enough for school he often went out on his own to play. He was very withdrawn and did not mix with other local children. At home he was often bad-tempered and Maja said that he occasionally went into fits of rage. Yet later in life he hardly ever got angry.

Einstein at school

Albert finally went to elementary school when he was seven years old, which was later than other children. Until then he had been taught at home by private tutors. He spent a lot of time on his own and didn't like playing sports, which his classmates thought was very odd.

At the time German schools were extremely strict. Children had to learn off by heart what was written in books or on the blackboard. Woe betide them if they didn't listen carefully and remember quickly. This method of learning did not suit Albert. In most classes he didn't make much effort, looked bored and took a long time to answer questions. His teachers described him as lazy and inattentive and assumed that he was stupid. He was often rapped over the knuckles with a ruler. However, Albert was good at maths and Latin, which he liked because they were logical subjects. Nonetheless, his Greek teacher once told him, "Nothing will ever become of you."

An interest in science

Albert found learning easier at home than at school. When he was five, he fell ill and had to spend weeks in bed. To stop him getting bored, his father gave him a compass to play with. Albert was fascinated by the way the needle swung round without being touched. He wondered what was pushing and pulling it. This may have been the experience that started him thinking about how the world around him worked.

A few years later his interest in science was encouraged by his uncle Jakob and by

Max Talmey, a medical student who was a regular visitor to his parents' home. Jakob taught him algebra and Max talked to him about the latest scientific ideas of the time, and about maths and philosophy. These talks established a pattern for Einstein. Throughout the rest of his life, he developed his theories by discussing his ideas and the ideas of other scientists with his friends.

When he was twelve, Albert moved from elementary school to a high school in Munich, the Luitpold Gymnasium. But his attitude to lessons didn't change. He loved maths, especially geometry, but was bored by all the other subjects he had to study and he hated the strict discipline. At home he began to teach himself advanced maths and physics and he also read books on philosophy.

Learning music

Pauline Einstein loved listening to music and also playing instruments herself. She decided that her young son should learn to play, too, and bought him a violin. At first, Albert didn't enjoy his music

◀ *A photograph from the archives of the city of Ulm showing Albert Einstein with his classmates at school. He is third from the right in the front row.*

11

lessons. His first music teacher left for good when Albert went into a wild tantrum as she tried to teach him. After mastering the violin, he moved on to the piano. He had a natural talent for the violin, and played it for most of his life to entertain himself, his friends and family. He said that playing helped him to think about his work and he carried his violin almost everywhere he went.

Albert gets religion

At German schools it was compulsory for children to learn about their own religion. Albert, like his parents, was Jewish. But nearly all the other children at school were Roman Catholics, and there was nobody at school who could teach Albert about Judaism. In the end he studied Judaism with one of his relatives. He became very religious, and even began to write songs about God. His parents were amazed. But after about a year his enthusiasm died down, and he went back to studying maths. When people asked Einstein if he believed in God, he said that the beauty and complexity of the universe made him think there must be some hidden force in control, but that he didn't believe in God.

Judaism

Judaism is the religion of the Jewish people. Their most sacred book is the Torah, or the five books of Moses. Judaism began more than 4,000 years ago. The father of the Jewish people was Abraham, who taught people to worship one God. Not all Jews practise Judaism. Albert's parents, for example, disliked the idea of organized religion. But anti-Semitic persecution made life difficult for all Jews, whether practising or not.

A move to Italy

In the early 1890s the Einsteins' business was failing again. There were plenty of customers in Munich, but plenty of competitors too, and they were short of work. Hermann did not seem worried, but it was obvious that they could not carry on losing money for much longer. Pauline's very wealthy parents offered to fund a new electrical business for Hermann and Jakob, but on one condition – that they moved to Italy to join them. The Einsteins accepted, and the family left Munich for Milan.

Albert was fifteen at the time. In order to go to a university, he needed his high-school exam certificate. So it was decided that he would stay in Munich on his own to complete his last year at high school, and take his exams at the end of it.

When the family left Munich, Albert moved into a boarding house. He soon began to feel abandoned and lonely. He hated being at school, and was not looking forward to doing military service afterwards, which was compulsory in Germany at that time. In despair, he went to see his doctor. The doctor wrote a letter to Albert's school saying that Albert was depressed. The only subject that really interested Albert was maths, and his maths teacher said he had taught Albert practically all he knew. So the headmaster agreed that Albert could leave, and Albert followed his parents to Italy. By doing so he effectively ceased to be a German citizen.

Studies in Zürich

When Albert was reunited with his family in Milan his depression soon lifted. But now he had a new problem. He was a high-school drop-out with no qualifications and no job. What was he going to do next?

For several months Albert didn't do very much at all, except meet up with the new friends he made in Milan, and, when the weather was good, go on trips to the nearby Alps.

Albert's father Hermann was concerned about his son. He kept badgering Albert to decide what he wanted to do with his life, and to make some firm plans. Finally Albert made his decision. He said that he wanted to study and teach philosophy. Hermann was not impressed. He said philosophy was a waste of time, and that Albert should get a proper, practical job like his own, being an electrical engineer.

Regardless of what he or his father wanted, Albert was stuck. He couldn't teach philosophy without a degree from a university and no university would accept a student without a high-school certificate. Reluctantly, Albert agreed to take a course in electrical engineering.

He chose to do it at one of the top technical colleges in Europe, the Federal Institute of Technology in Zürich, Switzerland. All he had to do to get in was to pass the college entrance exam.

Albert spent the next few months studying for the entrance exam and helping his father and uncle in the family engineering business (where his mathematical skills came in very useful). Just as he had at high school, Albert neglected the parts of the curriculum that he didn't enjoy, such as chemistry, biology and French. Although he attained fantastic marks in maths and science, he got low scores in everything else, and failed the exam overall. Luckily for Albert, the college professors, and Professor Heinrich Weber in particular, recognized that he had an outstanding

▶ *A portrait photo of Albert Einstein taken in 1895, around the time that he went to school in Switzerland to complete his high-school certificate.*

and natural gift for maths and science. They agreed that Albert would be allowed to enter the college the following year without re-taking the entrance exam. But there was one condition. Albert must pass his high-school certificate first.

Back to high school

There was nothing else for it. Albert would have to return to high school. The Einsteins chose a school in the town of Aarau, in a German-speaking area of Switzerland. It was arranged that Albert would stay with one of the school's teachers, Jost Winteler, and his family. Albert assumed that school life would be as unpalatable as it had been in Germany. But he was mistaken. The school was nothing like as strict as his old high school in Munich, and he found it far easier to learn.

Albert enjoyed his time in Aarau. The Wintelers had seven children, and Albert was treated just like another son. He played games with the younger children and went with the family on trips to the

▶ *A view of Zürich in 1900, the year before Albert became a Swiss citizen. His experience of school was happier in Switzerland than it had been in Germany.*

▲ *Albert Einstein with Mileva Maric, who became his first wife. The couple met at the Federal Institute of Technology. Einstein's mother did not approve of her.*

countryside. He found Switzerland's Alpine scenery very beautiful.

After school Einstein sat at the dining table and discussed maths and physics with Jost Winteler. Meanwhile he carried on teaching himself advanced mathematical techniques, and reading about the work of scientists and philosophers. He started to think about the very nature of the universe, about what matter could be made of, and about light, time and space, and how they could be related to each other. Thoughts such as these were to occupy his mind for the rest of his life.

At the end of his spell of school in Aarau, Albert got his usual mixture of good and bad exam results, but he passed his high-school certificate. He returned home to Milan and prepared to go off to college in Zürich.

Einstein in love

Einstein's friends from high school and college say that he was normally cheerful, had a good sense of humour, loved silly puns and enjoyed laughing. He was shy, but never afraid to get involved in an argument. He was also quite handsome, and met his first girlfriend in Aarau.

She was Marie, the Winterlers' daughter, who was two years older than Albert. They walked and talked together on family trips and played music together. After Albert left Aarau, they wrote to each other regularly, but he stopped writing soon after he moved to Zürich. Marie was very upset. Later, Albert's sister Maja married Marie's brother, but Albert always took care to avoid meeting Marie because he felt guilty about their break-up.

The reason Albert had stopped writing to Marie was that he had met and fallen in love with Mileva Maric, the woman who would eventually become his wife. She was the only woman in his class at the Federal Institute of Technology (at the time it was very unusual for women to study physics). When they met, he was eighteen and she was twenty-two.

Einstein the student

Einstein began studying at the Federal Institute of Technology in Zürich in 1897. He lived in a rented room in a house, where he often played music with the landlady's daughter. Before moving to Zürich, he had persuaded his parents that he wanted a job teaching physics. They had agreed that he could change courses from electrical engineering to physics.

Einstein was a disapproving student and not easy to teach. He didn't like most of the professors who taught him, and he let them know how he felt. He said they were self-important, too strict and that they thought that there were no new discoveries to be made in physics. He said they were afraid to hear about new theories because they didn't want their authority to be challenged. Einstein continually studied the latest scientific theories and discoveries. He thought he knew better than his teachers what he should be studying, so he went ahead and studied it on his own. He hardly ever went to any lectures, and made up his own experiments (one of which almost killed him when it went wrong). But he did just enough work to stop himself getting expelled from the college.

Not surprisingly, the professors did not think much of Einstein, either. They thought his attitude was bad and that he was a disruptive influence on the other students. He seemed to do almost no work, so they assumed he was lazy. They saw very little sign that Einstein was a genius in the making. Most of the professors didn't think he was clever enough to be at college at all. Professor Heinrich Weber, the man who had agreed that Einstein could enter the college without passing the entrance exam, felt very annoyed and was more disappointed with Einstein than anyone else. Worse still, Einstein kept calling him Herr Weber rather than Herr Professor, which was insulting. Weber told him, "You're clever, Einstein, extremely clever. But you have one great fault: you never let yourself be told anything!"

Although Einstein was hardly ever seen in a lecture room, he never stopped studying. He was very interested in and excited by the latest discoveries and theories in physics. He studied the work of top theoretical physicists, such as Michael Faraday (1791–1867), James Clerk Maxwell (1831–79) and Heinrich Hertz (1857–94). He also studied philosophy, and was especially impressed by the work of Ernst Mach (1838–1916). He was beginning to form his own ideas about the nature of matter and the universe. Even when he was relaxing he kept a notebook and pencil with him to scribble down his thoughts.

James Clerk Maxwell (1831–79) Heinrich Hertz (1857–94)

James Clerk Maxwell was a British theoretical physicist and one of the top scientists and mathematicians of the nineteenth century. He made many ground-breaking discoveries about electricity, light and the movement of molecules. But most importantly he wrote down laws linking electricity and magnetism, developing the work of Michael Faraday (1791–1867). He predicted that a whole range of electromagnetic waves exist, and that light was one of them. Maxwell's work was the starting point for much of modern physics.

Heinrich Hertz was a German scientist. Where Maxwell had predicted that electromagnetic waves exist, Hertz proved it by discovering radio waves and showing that they were electromagnetic waves similar to light. This was an important step in the development of radio communications, television and radar.

▶ *A portrait of James Clerk Maxwell, the British physicist, dating from 1875.*

◀ *Heinrich Hertz, the German scientist who discovered the existence of radio waves.*

Ernst Mach (1838–1916)

Ernst Mach was an Austrian physicist and philosopher. He studied how objects move through the air, creating shock waves. He also believed that all we know about science comes from our senses, and so might not necessarily be true. His work encouraged Einstein to re-think some of the theories that other scientists accepted as being true.

College friends

Although the professors at the Federal Institute of Technology had a low opinion of Einstein, his fellow students were very fond of him. They liked his sense of fun and happy laughter, his love of music and the fact that he ridiculed the professors behind their backs. Two of his closest student friends were Michele Besso, who studied engineering and often discussed theoretical physics with Einstein, and Marcel Grossman, who helped Einstein by giving him notes on the maths lectures that he didn't attend. These two would be valuable friends for the rest of Einstein's life. In fact, it was Grossman who was one of the first people

◄ *The Austrian physicist and philosopher Ernst Mach, photographed in 1872.*

to recognize that Einstein was a genius. Most of his other friends simply laughed when they heard of his plans to become a top physicist.

In 1900, after four years in Zürich, Albert, Mileva and the three other students in their class took their final exams. Albert came fourth in the class of five, and only just passed. Mileva came last. She was the only student to fail.

Work and marriage

After graduating in Zürich, Einstein returned to his parents' home in Milan. He took some news with him – Mileva had agreed to marry him.

Pauline Einstein had already decided that she did not like Mileva. She thought Mileva was too old, unhealthy and not very ladylike. She didn't think women should be scientists, and was suspicious about what Mileva wanted from her son. She told Albert that Mileva would ruin his life. Mileva knew how Pauline felt, because Einstein told her.

When he broke the news, his mother was horrified and said he should be marrying somebody better. Hermann was equally upset. He asked how Einstein thought he was going to look after himself and a wife with no job and no money. But Einstein was very stubborn. His parents' protests did not put him off. To cheer them up, he promised to learn about the family business so that he could take it over and run it himself one day.

While he was in Zürich, Einstein applied to become a Swiss citizen. This process took several years. Applicants had to fill in lengthy forms and answer questions about their personal lives. They were then investigated thoroughly by the Swiss authorities. Only people who would be useful citizens were successful. Einstein finally became a Swiss citizen in 1901. Having become a Swiss citizen, Einstein was required to do compulsory military service in the Swiss army. He really didn't want to go into the army, so he wasn't disappointed when he was rejected because the army doctors said he had flat feet. Now he was free to look for work. He thought it would be quite easy to get an assistant's job, either teaching at a college or university, or helping a scientist, so that is what he applied for. Professor Weber at the Federal Institute of Technology had even hinted to Einstein that he could become his assistant. In the end, Einstein probably blew his chances because of the way he treated Weber at college. Weber did not take him on after all, even though he needed assistants.

Einstein applied for several scientific posts in Switzerland and Germany, but had no success, and became depressed. It may have been that he gave Professor Weber as his referee in his applications, and Weber was unlikely to give Einstein a good reference. Or it may have been because he was Jewish, or because he was not born in Switzerland. Today, it seems amazing that the great Albert Einstein could not get a

▶ Albert Einstein as a young man, photographed in 1902 around the time of his appointment to the patent office in Bern.

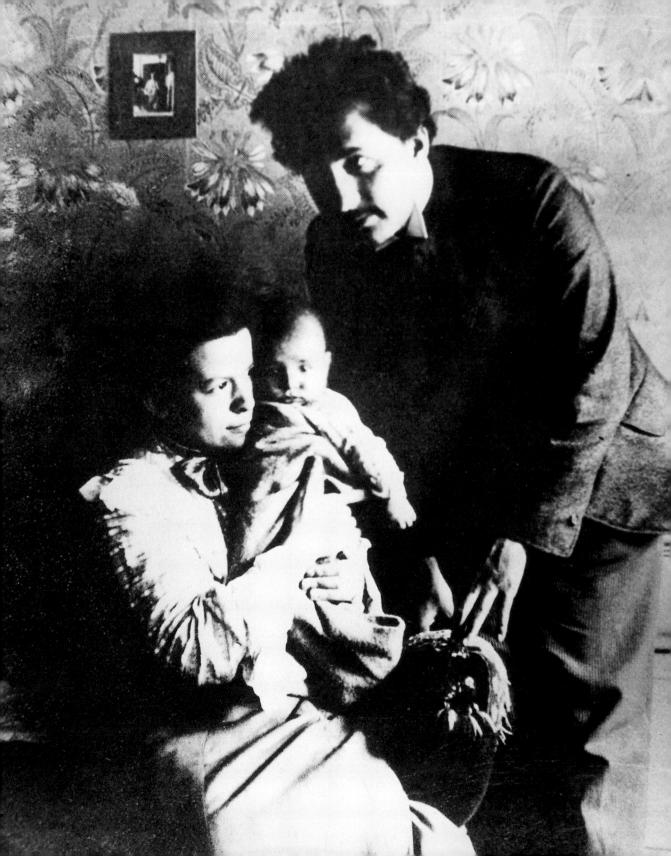

job. His father tried to help by writing secretly to the University of Leipzig asking for an assistant's job for his son.

Temporary jobs

Einstein moved back to Zürich to be with Mileva. They earned some money to live on by giving private lessons in maths and science. But before long Einstein ran out of money and had to return home to Italy once again.

Finally Einstein's luck changed. He got a temporary teaching job at a school in Winterthur, a town close to Zürich. Einstein turned out to be a good teacher. He enjoyed the job and was popular with his pupils. Soon after leaving Winterthur he got another job, teaching two pupils at a school in the town of Schaffhausen, also in Switzerland. He lodged with the school's head teacher, but the two men constantly argued and Albert was eventually fired.

Family matters

In the meantime, Mileva had re-taken her final exams at the Federal Institute of

◀ Albert and Mileva, photographed with their newborn son, Hans Albert, in Zürich in 1904.

Technology and failed again. She had also found out that she was pregnant. At that time, becoming pregnant without being married was frowned on. She and Albert could not let their parents know, so Mileva went into hiding away from Zürich so that the secret would not get out. The couple wrote to each other daily.

At the same time the Einsteins' family business was failing yet again. Hermann was so short of money that he asked Albert if he could help. Now it was critical for Einstein to get a full-time job. He needed to support himself, Mileva, his sister Maja and soon a baby, too. Albert and Mileva's daughter was born in the spring of 1902 at Mileva's family home in Novi Sad, in present-day Yugoslavia. They called her Lieserl. It was too difficult for Einstein to visit Novi Sad, and Mileva was too ill to return to Zürich. In the end, the baby was given up for adoption, and it is likely that Albert never even saw her.

In the autumn of 1902 Hermann Einstein died from heart disease; it's sad to think that Einstein's father never knew about his son's eventual fame. Hermann's death came as a great shock to Albert. He returned to Italy to see his father, and before he died, Hermann finally said he didn't mind if Albert married Mileva.

The couple were married in January 1903. Their first son, Hans Albert, was born in May 1904.

Einstein the patent clerk

Einstein's first full-time job was at the Swiss patent office in the city of Bern. His college friend Marcel Grossman knew the patent office director Friedrich Haller, and suggested that Einstein would be a good employee. In June 1902, just as he was running out of money again, Einstein got the job of third-class patent examiner. He examined new inventions sent to the office and decided which ones were original ideas and if they would work. He also wrote descriptions of the devices. He enjoyed the work because every day he came across new ideas and inventions.

Continuing studies

Ever since leaving college in Zürich, Einstein had continued his own studies in physics, reading the latest research produced by scientists such as Max Planck (1858–1947), and formulating his own ideas. Luckily, his job at the patent office allowed him plenty of spare time. Einstein's aims were very ambitious. He wanted to discover the laws that determine how matter behaves and how the universe works. Thoughts about this were constantly going round in his head. He discussed these ideas with his friends. Often he chatted with his college friend Michele Besso for days at a time about a particular problem. He worked even when he was looking after Hans Albert, rocking the cot with one hand and writing formulae with the other. Later he would publish these ideas in scientific papers. Einstein and some of his friends in Bern formed a group that met regularly to discuss physics and philosophy, and to socialize. They called themselves the Olympia Academy.

Max Planck (1858–1947)

Max Planck (right) was a German physicist who concluded that electromagnetic radiation can be thought of as tiny packets of energy, which he called quanta. This was the beginning of the science of quantum mechanics. Planck and Einstein worked together at Berlin University. Planck was awarded the Nobel Prize for physics in 1918.

A busy year

The year 1905, when Einstein was just 26 years old, was not only an eventful year in his life, but also an important year in the history of science. No one, not even other scientists, realized this until a few years later.

At the time only a few close friends had any idea what Einstein was working on, or that he had developed theories that answered some of the major scientific puzzles of the day. These would prove to be theories that would transform the way people thought about physics for ever.

During 1905 Einstein wrote four major scientific papers. He sent them for publication to a German scientific journal called *Annalen der Physik* (*Annals of Physics*), which was read by hundreds of scientists. The journal's editorial director was Max Planck, whose own research Einstein had studied. Einstein's first paper was an explanation of the photoelectric effect (see below). The second was about measuring the size of molecules, for which Einstein received his doctorate from the University of Zürich. The third was an explanation of Brownian motion (see below). The fourth

paper, published in September 1905, was the most radical. Its proper title was "On the Electrodynamics of Moving Bodies", but it became known as the theory of special relativity. It claimed that the laws of motion that scientists had relied on for more than two hundred years were not true. A few weeks later, Einstein published a short addition to this paper. It included the famous equation $E=mc^2$.

Physics in the 1800s

To understand why Einstein worked on the theories he did, and why they were so important, we have to understand how much physicists knew at the time, and what new discoveries they were making. Scientists used the laws of motion and gravitation worked out by Isaac Newton

▶ *Sir Isaac Newton (1642–1727) went to Trinity College, Cambridge, and spent his life ceaselessly investigating mathematics, optics, chronology, chemistry, theology, mechanics, dynamics and the occult. His achievements are virtually countless.*

(1642–1727) way back in the 1600s. These laws are used to predict how objects move and how bodies in space such as planets and moons move around their orbits. They also believed that light travelled in waves, like ripples on a pond.

In the 1860s James Clerk Maxwell had predicted that electromagnetic waves existed, and he said that light was a type of electromagnetic wave. In the 1880s Heinrich Hertz had discovered radio waves, which showed that Maxwell's theory was right. But nobody knew how electromagnetic waves got from place to place. And experiments seemed to show that the way the waves behaved did not fit in with Newton's laws after all. The atomic theory of the time said that all matter is made up of atoms, but nobody had seen an atom, so it was still only a theory. Radioactivity had been discovered, but nobody knew where it came from. Scientists such as Marie Curie (1867–1934) were trying to find out. Einstein's theories provided answers to some of these difficult problems.

◀ *Marie Curie (1867–1934), a Polish-born scientist who, with her French-born scientist husband, Pierre, investigated radioactivity, discovering the elements polonium and radium in 1898. She won the Nobel Prize for chemistry in 1911 for her work on radium.*

Electromagnetic waves

Light, radio waves, microwaves, X-rays and infra-red rays are all types of electromagnetic waves. The whole family of waves is called the electromagnetic spectrum. All these waves travel through space at the speed of light, which is almost 300,000 kilometres per second. Electromagnetic waves are also called electromagnetic radiation. Sometimes scientists treat electromagnetic waves as waves, but sometimes they treat them as streams of particles instead.

Einstein and the photoelectric puzzle

Electrons are tiny particles that are part of atoms. When light hits a piece of metal, electrons are knocked off the atoms at the surface of the metal. This is called the photoelectric effect. We make use of the photoelectric effect in electronic devices that detect light, such as the sensors on doors that open automatically. In 1905, scientists knew about the photoelectric effect, but nobody could explain how it worked.

Einstein came up with a completely new theory about light in order to explain the photoelectric effect. He imagined light as a stream of particles instead of a

Planck and quanta

Einstein's idea of photons was inspired by an idea of Max Planck's that light and other electromagnetic radiation are emitted in chunks called quanta, rather than evenly in a continuous stream. Einstein imagined, in the case of light, for example, that quanta were in the form of extremely tiny mass-less particles.

wave. He called the particles photons, and said that they were not solid objects, but like little bullets of energy. If a photon had enough energy, he said, it would knock an electron from its atom. Nobody accepted the theory until 1913, when experiments showed that Einstein was right. In 1921, Einstein eventually received a Nobel Prize for his work on the photoelectric effect.

Brownian motion

If you drop very tiny particles, such as pollen grains, into a liquid and look at them through a microscope, you can see the grains jiggling about. This jiggling is called Brownian motion and is named after botanist Robert Brown (1773–1858), who first noticed it in 1827. Scientists were baffled by Brownian motion and couldn't work out what was pushing and pulling the grains to make them move.

Einstein, however, was fascinated and was the first to explain it. He said that the tiny molecules (groups of atoms) that make up a liquid are moving about all the time because of their heat energy. They keep bashing into the pollen grains from different directions, causing them to jiggle about. Einstein's explanation of Brownian motion helped to convince many scientists that atoms really do exist.

Einstein's imagination

Einstein's theory of special relativity was an original and extraordinary idea. He came up with it for two reasons. The first was that he was not totally convinced by the theories that other scientists had accepted for many years as being absolutely accurate. He didn't say that the theories believed by scientists were completely wrong, just that they might not be completely right. Einstein asked himself the sort of questions about matter and the universe that other scientists thought had already been answered long before.

The second reason was that he did not accept that what appeared to be happening was in fact what was actually taking place. His studies of philosophy helped him to pose questions using this method and it was this original way of thinking that made Einstein the genius he was. He once summed up his attitude by saying, "Imagination is more important than knowledge." He also argued that "education should train the mind to think, not fill it with facts."

The theory of special relativity links together movement, light, space and time. Einstein had been thinking about this and discussing it with his friends since he was sixteen and still at high school. He said that although it had been going round in his head for so long, the answer came to him one morning in a flash of inspiration. Einstein had no experimental evidence to help him, so the theory was genuinely the product of his imagination combined with his philosophical method of questioning and thinking things through.

The theory of special relativity

The paper that Einstein sent to the journal *Annals of Physics* was 31 pages long, and full of complex mathematical equations.

The theory of special relativity itself is far too complex and advanced to explain accurately here. However, we can try to understand how Einstein developed the theory, what it predicted and why his work on it was so important for physics. We'll start by looking at the ideas in those days about space and time.

Relative motion

Scientists use the word velocity as a measurement of speed and direction. We usually measure velocity compared to (in other words, "relative to") an observer standing still on the Earth's surface. Imagine a car travelling at 80 km/h north along a straight road. Its velocity is 80 km/h in a northerly direction. Now imagine a second car on the same road, this time with a velocity of 100 km/h in a northerly direction. To an observer in this second car, the first car appears to be going backwards. Its velocity relative to this observer is 20 km/h in a southerly direction.

The ether and fixed space

In the early 1900s physicists did not understand how light (and all the other electromagnetic waves) travelled. They didn't think light could travel through a vacuum (as there is in space), so they imagined that the universe must be filled with something invisible that carried the waves. They called it the ether.

The ether was thought to be completely still, and all the objects in space were supposed to move through it. The idea was that the ether made space fixed or "absolute". Scientists thought they could measure the velocity of any object in the universe relative to the fixed ether, just as we measure the speed of a car relative to the Earth's surface.

▶ *The room in the house in Bern in which Einstein perfected his theory of relativity. His music stand and his constant companion, the violin, are shown as well. Einstein loved to play Mozart in his spare time.*

◄ *Albert Abraham Michelson (1852–1931) was a German-born American physicist and was the winner of the 1907 Nobel Prize for physics. He invented the Michelson interferometer, which made precise measurements of the speed of light. He was the first to make measurements of the stars.*

► *Edward Williams Morley (1838–1923) was an American chemist and physicist. He tried to achieve ever more precise and accurate measurements. His early research was on the oxygen content of air. He then moved on to study the relative atomic mass of oxygen. Later, he worked with Michelson (above left).*

The ether disappears

In 1887 two American scientists, Michelson and Morley, tried to prove that the ether existed by measuring the speed of light in different directions across the Earth's surface. They thought that light must travel like any other object, as described in Newton's laws of motion.

Imagine a ball thrown forwards from a moving train. The ball travels through the air at the speed of the throw plus the speed of the train. Michelson and Morley thought the Earth was moving through the ether, like a train through the air. They thought the speed of light from a lamp going in the same direction as the Earth would be faster than the speed of light from a lamp going in the opposite direction. The results of their experiments didn't bear this out. Light seemed to travel at the same speed in all directions. No one could work out what was going on.

Einstein's assumptions

Einstein tried to imagine himself sitting on a beam of light and travelling with it. He wondered if the light would enter his eyes or if the source of the light would disappear. And if he carried a mirror with him, would the light from his face be able to catch up with the mirror? If it couldn't, then his reflection would disappear. Einstein's instinct was that his reflection would look normal. It shouldn't matter how fast you were going, he said; things travelling at the same velocity as you should look normal. If this was true, then if you were moving very fast, Newton's laws didn't work. Einstein realized that a new set of laws of motion was needed.

Einstein assumed two things to start with. The first was that the laws of physics must be the same for everything, no matter what their velocity relative to each other. Einstein didn't see why the laws should change just because things were moving. His second assumption was that the speed of light is the same for everything, no matter what its velocity. This is what the Michelson–Morley experiment seemed to show.

Einstein also said that the ether did not exist and wasn't needed for light to be able to travel. This statement also meant there was no fixed space. Instead, it meant that the universe is only made up of objects moving relative to each other. He said you can't measure movement relative to space, but only relative to

The principle of relativity

The word relativity was not a new one to scientists. They had used it for hundreds of years. They knew that if you are moving in a straight line at a constant speed, you can't actually tell that you are moving unless you can see something that you can compare your movement to. This is called the principle of relativity. For example, imagine that you are in a car that is moving very smoothly along a straight road. If you don't look out of the windows at the scenery going past, you can't tell that the car is moving.

another object. This means, for example, that you can never say something is absolutely still, but only that it is still relative to another object in space.

Changing space and time

Imagine you are standing at the side of a straight road at night. Farther along the road is a stationary car, facing you with its headlamps on. Light from the headlamps travels away from the car at the speed of light, as measured by an observer in the car, and it reaches you at the speed of light, too. Now imagine that the car starts moving towards you. The light still leaves the car at the speed of light, measured by

the observer in the car. You might think that it would reach you at the speed of light plus the speed of the car. No, said Einstein, the speed of light is fixed. The light reaches you at the speed of light, no matter how fast the car approaches. The car itself could be travelling at nearly the speed of light.

Even Einstein had problems imagining what this all meant. Until then, everybody assumed that space was fixed, that time always went past at the same rate, flowing from past to future, and that the speed of light could change. Einstein concluded that if the speed of light was constant, then if one thing was moving relative to another, space and time must change instead. He also realized that two events that appear to happen at exactly the same time to one observer could appear to happen at different times to another.

The speed of light

Einstein said that light always travels through a vacuum at the same speed, and that it never changes, no matter what the speed of the source of light is. The speed of light, which is given the symbol c, is 299,792 kilometres per second. A beam of light (if it could bend enough) would get round the Earth's equator in about one tenth of a second.

▶ According to Einstein's theory of special relativity there is no absolute time. Time is a function of planetary motion and so no unit of time is independent of its reference frame. A clock within a moving reference frame (represented by the flying alarm clocks) shows a different time from a clock in a stationary time frame (represented by the grandfather clock).

A famous equation

Einstein's theory of special relativity gave equations that showed what an observer would see when moving relative to other objects.

These equations included some developed by Hendrik Lorentz (1853–1928), known as Lorentz transformations. They showed how time and space seem to change for observers moving relative to each other.

The equations predict that a moving object looks shorter than a stationary object. For example, to an observer at the roadside, a moving car looks shorter than a stationary car. And the faster the car goes, the shorter it appears to be. But to an observer in the moving car, the car appears perfectly normal.

The equations also predict that time appears to slow down on a moving object. So to the observer on the roadside, the hands of a clock in the moving car would appear to slow down. The faster the car goes, the more time slows down. This effect is called time dilation. To an observer in the moving car, time passes normally. The effects of changes of length and time dilation are infinitesimally small unless an object is moving at extremely high speeds (see panel on p 45). At the sorts of speeds that everyday objects (even the very fastest aircraft) move on Earth, the changes are simply not large enough for us to see. In practice, our car would have to be travelling at many thousands of times its normal speed for the changes in length and time to become noticeable, and then, of course, it would be almost impossible to see the car, let alone judge its length and watch its clock as it whizzed by!

Finally, the equations predict that the mass of a moving object appears greater than a stationary object. The faster it goes, the greater its mass appears to grow. Einstein's prediction comes true in experimental facilities called particle

▶ *Hendrik Antoon Lorentz (1853–1928), Dutch physicist, photographed in the year 1902. In that same year he, along with P Zeeman, won the 1902 Nobel Prize for Physics for his prediction of the Zeeman effect. He based his work on the equations of J C Maxwell (see page 21) to explain the reflection and refraction of light and proposed his electron theory.*

...s Unendliche, wenn sich q dem Werte ...

...nendlichen Energie-Aufwandes, ...

...dgkeit c zu erteilen. Um zu sehen, dass d...

...hwindigkeit in den von Newtons Mech...

...n wir den Nenner $\overset{\text{nach Potenzen von } \frac{q^2}{c^2}}{}$ und erhalten

$$\mathcal{E} = m c^2 + \frac{m}{2} q^2 + \dots \qquad (28')$$

... Glied der rechten Seite ist der geläu...

...klassischen Mechanik. Was bedeutet aber ...

...ses hat zwar streng genommen hier keine ...

...8) eine additive Konstante willkürlich ...

...em Blick auf (28), dass das Glied $m c^2$ ...

... $\frac{m}{2} q^2$ untrennbar verbunden ist. Man ...

...telle dazu, diesen Term $m c^2$ eine reale ...

...k für ...

...ergie des ruhenden Punktes anzusehen ...

...usse einen $\mathcal{E}$ ~~der totale Energie~~ hätten ...

...ne m als einen Energievorrat von der Grö...

... Körpers). ~~Ist diese Auffassung getroffen~~ ...

...rs können wir aber ändern, z. B. inde...

... $m c^2$ stets der Ruhe-Energie des Körp...

...der träge Masse des Körpers...

Only at high speeds

The changes of space, time and mass predicted in Einstein's theory of special relativity are only really noticeable at speeds approaching the speed of light. Einstein worked out an equation that predicts how mass increases with speed. Here's an example of what it predicts.

Imagine a car weighing 1,000 kg. At 500,000 km/h its mass goes up by only a tenth of a gram! Even at half the speed of light its mass is only 1,155 kg. But at 99 per cent of the speed of light its mass increases to more than 50,000 kg. This means that Newton's laws still work most of the time.

accelerators. Here, sub-atomic particles that are accelerated to more than 99 per cent of the speed of light increase in mass over a hundred times.

An amusing idea

A few weeks after completing the theory of special relativity, Einstein realized that he had left something out. So he sent a three-page addition for publication. It included what has become the most

◀ This is the general theory of relativity as written in Einstein's own hand. Shown here is page 39 of the 72-page manuscript in which, in 1912, Einstein explained his theory of relativity for the first time.

famous equation in science. It was $E=mc^2$. Einstein had worked out this equation from the equations in the theory of special relativity. It is incredibly simple, but also incredibly important.

The equation means that mass (m) and energy (E) are the same thing, and that mass can be changed into energy and energy changed into mass. Before this, every scientist was sure that mass was one thing and energy was a completely different thing. Now Einstein was saying they were the same. It meant, in theory, that any object could be turned into energy. Even Einstein himself was amazed by the idea. He said: "This thought is amusing and infectious but I cannot possibly know whether the good Lord

$E = mc^2$

The equation reads "E equals m c squared". It means that the energy (E) in an object is equal to the object's mass (m) multiplied by the speed of light (c) squared (multiplied by itself). If you do the sum for a mass of one kilogram, you find the energy in it is $1 \times (300,000)^2$ = 90,000 million million joules. That much energy would run 30 million 100-watt light bulbs for a year.

Mass and inertia

If you try to make an object move or speed up, it seems to resist. This resistance to motion is called inertia. We measure inertia by mass, in kilograms (kg). The greater an object's mass, the bigger its inertia, and the harder it is to get moving. So a car with a mass of 1,000 kg is harder to move than a bike of 30 kg.

does not laugh at it and has led me up the garden path."

Here's an explanation of how the theory of special relativity shows how energy and mass are the same thing. Einstein's equations predict that the mass of an object appears to get larger and larger as it gets nearer to the speed of light.

Imagine that you could keep pushing on a car to make it accelerate to higher and higher speeds. You need energy from your muscles to do this. At low speeds, this energy would be turned into movement energy in the car. According to Einstein, as the car approached the speed of light, its mass would start to get very big indeed. Pushing would now get very hard, and each push would make the car go only a tiny bit faster, but a tiny

increase in speed would make its mass increase a lot. So the energy you used to push would have been turned into mass. Einstein concluded that mass must be energy in a different form.

Einstein's equations predict that an object's mass would become infinite at the speed of light, which is not physically possible. This means that nothing can actually reach the speed of light, except light and other electromagnetic waves. Einstein concluded that the speed of light is the maximum possible speed. It is the speed limit in the universe.

Energy from mass

The equation $E = mc^2$ was a possible explanation for the effect of radioactivity, which had been discovered a few years before. Einstein said the equation showed how a huge amount of energy in the form of radiation could come from a small piece of radioactive material. He predicted that the mass of a piece of radioactive material must decrease by a tiny amount as it gave off radiation.

▶ *Einstein's theories about physics and the nature of the universe involve complicated equations that are usually only understood by other scientists.*

$$\sum \frac{1}{\sqrt{1-u^2}} = \sum \frac{1}{\sqrt{1-\bar{u}^2}}$$

$$\sum \frac{u_i}{\sqrt{1-\bar{u}^2}} = \sum \frac{u_i}{\sqrt{1-u^2}}$$

$$\mathcal{E} = \mathcal{E}_0' + m\left(\frac{1}{\sqrt{1-u^2}} - 1\right)$$

En. L. K': $\quad 2\mathcal{E}_0 + 2m\left(\frac{1}{\sqrt{1-u'^2}} - 1\right) = 2\bar{\mathcal{E}}_0 + 2\bar{m}\left(\frac{1}{\sqrt{1-\bar{u}'^2}}\cdots\right)$

En. L. K: $\quad 2\mathcal{E}_0 + m\left(\frac{1}{\sqrt{1-u^2}} - 1\right) + m\left(\frac{1}{\sqrt{1-u^2}} - 1\right) = 2\bar{\mathcal{E}}_0 \cdots$

$$\mathcal{E}_0 - m + \frac{m}{\sqrt{1-u'^2}\sqrt{1-v^2}} = \bar{\mathcal{E}}_0 - \bar{m} + \frac{\bar{m}}{\sqrt{1-\bar{u}'^2}\sqrt{1-v^2}}$$

$$\mathcal{E}_0 - m + \frac{m}{\sqrt{1-u'^2}} = \bar{\mathcal{E}}_0 - \bar{m} + \frac{\bar{m}}{\sqrt{1-\bar{u}'^2}}$$

$$\left[(\bar{\mathcal{E}}_0 - \mathcal{E}_0) - (\bar{m} - m)\right]\left(\frac{1}{\sqrt{1-v^2}} - 1\right) = 0$$

$$\neq 0$$

$$\Delta \mathcal{E}_0 = \Delta m$$

$$\mathcal{E}_0 = m$$

Nuclear power

A practical application of the famous equation E=mc² can be seen at a nuclear power station. When an atom splits in two (a process called nuclear fission), some mass disappears and is turned into heat energy. In a nuclear power station, this energy is converted into electricity for homes, offices and factories. Nuclear power is also used for propulsion in some large military ships and submarines, and to produce electricity on space probes. The drawbacks of nuclear power are accidental release of radioactive waste and the problems of long-term storage of used radioactive fuel.

Einstein was proved to be right by experiments carried out in 1930. These showed that energy in the form of electromagnetic radiation and heat is released when particles leave the nucleus of an atom. This change in the nucleus is called a nuclear reaction. The mass of the nucleus and the particles after the reaction is always a tiny amount less than

▶ *Einstein's work in physics paved the way for the development of nuclear power stations. This is the Chinon Nuclear Power Station at Indre-et–Loire, in France. Chinon's first reactor began working in 1964, and the the last reactor unit was decommissioned in 1990.*

it was before. This mass is turned into energy in the reaction. Energy is also released when the nucleus of an atom splits in two. This sort of nuclear reaction is called nuclear fission. It releases enormous amounts of energy in nuclear power stations and nuclear weapons. In 1905, though, Einstein did not know that nuclear fission would be possible.

Reactions to relativity

Einstein had worked hard to complete his theory of special relativity. After sending it to the *Annals of Physics* for publication, he stayed in bed for a few days to recover. Then he took a holiday with Mileva and Hans Albert, now two years old, to visit Mileva's parents, whom he had never met. On their return to Bern, Einstein went back to work at the patent office. In 1906 he was promoted to "technical expert second class", with a slightly better salary.

Einstein eagerly awaited responses from the scientific community to his theory of special relativity. He thought there would be an instant reaction to his revolutionary

◀ *Another portrait of Max Planck, the German physicist, taken in 1905. His quantum theory, along with the theory of relativity, brought physics into the modern era. He won the Nobel Prize in 1918.*

ideas. But there were none, at least not immediately. This was because the many scientists who read the theory either thought that the ideas in it were very strange, or even ridiculous, or they simply couldn't understand them.

Finally, there was some reaction. Max Planck, then at the University of Berlin and already a renowned scientist, wrote to Einstein, asking some questions about relativity theory. Einstein quickly replied, but then things went quiet again. He was extremely disappointed. Nobody seemed to be interested in the theories that had taken him many years of hard work and inspiration to develop.

Slowly, things began to change, largely owing to Max Planck. In 1906 Planck sent his assistant to visit Einstein to get a further explanation. The assistant went away and wrote a scientific paper about relativity, and Planck talked about Einstein's ideas in his university lectures.

In 1907, with his work published and interest growing, Einstein decided to try to get a university teaching job. But his first attempt failed. After asking for an unpaid lecturer's job at Bern University, he was rejected because the head of physics couldn't understand relativity.

The theory of general relativity

In 1909, Einstein was finally offered the academic teaching job he had wanted for so long. He resigned from the patent office in Bern to become professor of theoretical physics at Zürich University.

While the patent office director was disappointed to lose such a good patent clerk, anti-Semitism had reared its ugly head at the university, almost preventing Einstein from getting the position as professor. The selection panel there had not been keen on appointing a Jewish professor and Einstein only managed to get the appointment because Professor Kleiner, the head of physics at the university, supported him. Kleiner thought Einstein was one of the best young theoretical physicists around.

Albert and Mileva were happy to be back in Zürich, where they had plenty of friends. Luckily they found themselves living next to Friedrich Adler, an old friend of Einstein's from the Federal Institute of Technology. Einstein often discussed his latest ideas with Adler.

Mileva was pregnant again, and their second son, named Eduard, was born in July 1910.

To Prague and back

Despite being settled in Zürich, Einstein soon applied for the job of professor of theoretical physics at the German University in Prague in the present-day Czech Republic. He delayed the move once after his students in Zürich begged him to stay, but he eventually went to Prague in 1911.

By now other scientists were beginning to take Einstein's theories more seriously and he was invited to lecture at other universities in Europe. One of these visits

▶ *A portrait of Albert Einstein dating from 1918, by which time he was a professor at Berlin University. 1918 was also the year that World War One ended.*

took him to Leiden in the Netherlands. Here he met and stayed with one of his heroes, Hendrik Lorentz, whose equations Einstein had used in special relativity.

Einstein had mixed feelings about Prague. The research facilities at the German University were excellent, and the pay allowed him and Mileva to rent a good apartment and hire a maid. On the other hand, he had to spend a great deal of time on experiments and administration, which left less opportunity for his own studies. Illness and disease were common in Prague,

which made him and Mileva worry about the boys, and he found the people there unfriendly.

So Einstein was delighted when, in June 1912, his old college friend Michele Grossman offered him the job of professor of mathematical physics at the Federal Institute of Technology, back in Zürich. Einstein was warmly welcomed back to the college where he had been a disruptive student fifteen years before.

The Einsteins had not been in Zürich long when Max Planck tried to persuade Einstein to join him as a professor at Berlin University. Einstein eventually went to Berlin at the end of 1913. Planck set up the Kaiser Wilhelm Physical Institute at the university specially for Einstein, so that Einstein could carry on his research on relativity. He was given no teaching duties, and was required to lecture only occasionally. Einstein's reputation as a scientist grew. In 1913, Einstein was voted into a group of elite scientists called the Prussian Academy of Sciences. At this time he decided to resume his German citizenship.

◀ A family photograph of Mileva and her sons. Eduard is on her right and Hans Albert stands behind her.

Einstein the lecturer

At university, Einstein's style of lecturing was quite different from other professors'. The students were amazed when he turned up in scruffy clothes with his lecture notes scribbled on a few scraps of paper. But they found what Einstein had to say very interesting. His lectures were very informal, and he encouraged students to interrupt him to ask questions. And he always found time to answer them, even if it meant going with the students to a café or to his home after the lecture. When Einstein became world famous, he often gave lectures to the general public. They may not have understood his complex theories (after all, even many learned scientists didn't), but they did enjoy the humorous and friendly way in which he presented them.

More family problems

Although his job was going well, Einstein had family problems. Mileva wasn't happy. She had not wanted to leave her friends in Zürich to move to Prague or to Berlin, and she and Albert were not getting on well. She said that Albert was more interested in his work than he was in her. He was always bringing home

World War One

World War One broke out in the summer of 1914. One of the main reasons for the war was that Germany's military leaders wanted their nation to become the most powerful country in Europe. When the war finally ended in the autumn of 1918, with Germany defeated, ten million people were dead, including two million German soldiers.

Einstein hated war and was distressed when World War One began. He criticized the German emperor, Emperor Wilhelm, for his military aggression. During the war, he campaigned for peace by handing out leaflets in Berlin.

students to talk to or friends to play music with, and husband and wife hardly spoke to each other. In addition, she and Einstein's mother still did not like each other. In 1914, soon after Mileva and the two boys arrived in Berlin to join Albert, the marriage broke down. Mileva moved back to Zürich, taking the boys with her. The outbreak of World War One made travelling difficult, so it was hard for Albert and Mileva to meet to discuss

▶ *A scene from the Battle of Vauxaillon (14–15 September 1918) on the Western Front. German soldiers are shown retreating as Germany surrenders.*

their problems. In the end they separated for good. Einstein saw the boys during their holidays, wrote to them regularly and sent money for them and Mileva.

One of the reasons for the separation was a woman called Elsa Löwenthall, the daughter of Einstein's father's cousin. She and Albert had met in the spring of 1912, and had secretly started writing to each other. They began seeing each other when Einstein moved to Berlin. In 1917, Einstein fell ill. He collapsed and gradually lost weight. Doctors finally found out that he had a stomach ulcer. He spent weeks in bed but, as always, he kept working. He was ill again the following year, this time with jaundice. On both occasions Elsa looked after him.

A happy thought

Einstein's 1905 theory was called "special" relativity because it was only true for objects that moved at a steady velocity. In the theory the objects were not allowed to accelerate, which means they could not change speed or direction. Now he was working on a theory of general relativity. This would be true for

◀ *Einstein (far left) and his colleagues at Berlin University, photographed in 1918.*

objects that were accelerating because of gravity. The task Einstein had set himself was to link space, time, light and gravity together. This undertaking was many times more difficult than the development of the theory of special relativity.

Einstein had begun thinking about general relativity soon after completing his theory of special relativity. In 1907 he had what he called the "happiest thought of my life". He realized that the acceleration of an object by gravity appears to be the same as any other

The Principle of Equivalence

Here's how Einstein explained the Principle of Equivalence. Imagine you are in a lift in a building, and the lift is still. You can feel the lift floor pushing upwards on you because gravity pulls you downwards.

Now imagine that the lift is in the middle of space far from any stars or planets, where there is no gravity. If the lift accelerates upwards, the lift floor pushes upwards on you, which is exactly what you felt before. Therefore, said Einstein, an observer in a lift, who can't see out, can't tell the difference between the effects of gravity and the effects of acceleration.

▲ *Mass distorts space-time in the same way a ball distorts a rubber sheet. Here's a model of the Sun and Earth. Distortion of the sheet (i.e. space-time) by "Sun" makes "Earth" roll around it.*

acceleration, and that gravity and acceleration must therefore be the same thing. Einstein called this the Principle of Equivalence (see panel on p 59). It was an important step in his theory of general relativity.

Einstein carried on working on his theory for many years. Finally, in 1915, after a period when he worked extremely hard for several weeks, getting little sleep, eating simple meals and giving no lectures, he finally completed the theory. He sent it to the *Annals of Physics*, where it was published in 1916.

Predictions of general relativity

Newton's laws say that gravity is a force of attraction between two objects. This force depends on the masses of the objects and the distance between them. For example, Newton's laws say that an object falls to Earth because the object and Earth are attracted to one another.

Einstein disagreed – he said that gravity was not a force at all. Instead, gravity is caused by distortions of space and time. He said that mass affects space-time, and that space-time affects motion. The bigger the mass, the bigger the distortions. So an object falls to Earth because of the shape of space, not because of any force. Einstein also said that the Earth orbits the Sun because this is the shortest path through the distorted space created by the huge mass of the Sun. It was a mind-boggling idea and difficult to imagine.

In 1911, Einstein realized that his ideas for general relativity meant that the motion of light and other electromagnetic waves would be affected by mass. The light would follow the shortest path through space near the mass, which would not be a straight line. The effects would only be noticeable if light passed very close to a very big mass, such as a star.

General relativity was still only a theory. Only a few other scientists could follow the hugely complicated maths in it. In fact, Einstein reckoned that only a dozen people in the world would understand it. Others reacted as they had reacted to the theory of special relativity. They said the whole idea of distorted space and time was nonsense. There was nothing Einstein could do to persuade them until there was some experimental proof for general relativity. This finally arrived in 1919.

The motion of Mercury

Mercury is the planet closest to the Sun. Its orbit is the shape of a squashed circle, called an ellipse. But each year the ellipse itself moves round the Sun a bit. This had been noticed in the 1840s, but could not be explained. However, general relativity showed the movement of the ellipse was caused by tiny distortions of time and space produced by Mercury's high orbital speed and closeness to the Sun.

World fame

After separating from Mileva in 1916, Einstein asked her for a divorce. Einstein promised her that if he ever won the Nobel Prize, he would give the prize money to Mileva and the boys. When Mileva realized that there was no chance of a reconciliation, she reluctantly agreed.

Einstein and Mileva were divorced in 1919 but Einstein continued to visit Zürich to see Hans Albert and Eduard. In the summer of 1919, Einstein married Elsa Löwenthall. He moved into her apartment with her two daughters, Ilsa and Margot.

In 1925, Einstein's son Hans Albert, who was 22 at the time, said he wanted to marry an older woman. Einstein was very worried. He did not want Hans Albert to make the same mistakes he had made. He tried to talk Hans Albert out of the marriage, but he failed. Hans Albert married and became an engineer. Eventually he moved to the USA, where he became professor of engineering at the University of California.

As a child, his younger son Eduard was very shy and often ill. Einstein thought he had inherited a mental illness, as Mileva's sister was mentally ill. But Eduard's friends and teachers said he got on well at school. In 1930 Eduard suffered a mental breakdown. He wrote to Einstein, accusing his father of deserting him, and blaming him for his life being in ruins. Einstein was very upset. Unfortunately, Eduard spent most of the rest of his life in a home for the mentally ill in Switzerland.

In 1920 Einstein's mother Pauline became ill with cancer. She moved to Berlin to be with Einstein, and died soon after.

The eclipse of 1919

To prove his theory of general relativity, Einstein knew that he would have to show that light was bent near a massive object. His opportunity to do this was to

▶ *Einstein with his second wife, Elsa, photographed in 1928, the year before his 50th birthday. He and Elsa had been married nearly ten years.*

An eclipse of the Sun

An eclipse of the Sun, or solar eclipse, happens every few years when the Moon moves in line with the Earth and the Sun, and casts a shadow on the Earth. For a few minutes, from certain places on Earth, the Moon appears to just cover the Sun. This is called a total eclipse. During an eclipse like this, astronomers can see the edges of the Sun without being blinded by its brightness.

observe whether light from a distant star passing close to the Sun on its way to the Earth was bent as it passed the Sun. This bending would make the star appear to change position very slightly. Einstein knew that the only time to see this would be during a total eclipse of the Sun, when the brightness of the Sun would be blocked by the Moon.

Einstein had to wait until World War One was over before his theory could be tested. The next eclipse after the war was due on 29 May 1919. Einstein had sent a

◀ *This is the total solar eclipse of 11 July 1991. In this image, a few pinkish flares can be seen in the bright corona (top, bottom and centre right of the disc). The bright patch of light on the lower right is a small part of the solar disc visible at the edge of the Moon. This is known as the "diamond ring effect".*

copy of his theory to Sir Arthur Eddington (1882–1944), the Plumian Professor of Astronomy at Cambridge University. Along with Sir Frank Dyson, the British Astronomer Royal, Eddington organized a scientific expedition to Guinea in Africa, to observe the eclipse, and to take photographs.

The expedition recorded the eclipse in a series of 16 photographs. It took many weeks for Eddington and Dyson to process and examine the photographic plates. One of the photographs, along with some others of the eclipse taken in South America, showed that stars whose light shaved the edge of the Sun had appeared to change position. The change was almost the exact amount that Einstein had predicted (more accurate experiments in the 1970s showed he was, in fact, exactly right). It appeared to show that Einstein's theory of general relativity was correct.

Reactions to the news

The good news reached Einstein in September 1919 in a telegram from Hendrik Lorentz. It read: "Eddington found star displacement at Sun." The Royal Society and the Royal

Astronomical Society, both in London, described Einstein's theory of general relativity as "one of greatest achievements in the history of human thought…"

Hitting the headlines

Until now Einstein's name was known only by his fellow scientists. Suddenly he became the most famous scientist on the planet. Newspaper reporters and photographers all wanted to interview and photograph him. He received thousands of letters and was asked to write articles and give lectures about his theories. Dozens of newborn babies were even named Albert after him. Einstein was surprised and embarrassed by all the attention and he didn't like being in the public eye. He was also a little annoyed that it prevented him from getting on with his work as he wanted.

Not all the reaction was positive, however. Some scientists said the evidence from the eclipse was not proof of general relativity. They said that there could be other explanations for bending

◀ *A portrait of Sir Arthur Eddington (1882–1944), mathematician and astrophysicist, drawn in 1929. He was a professor at Cambridge University.*

light. Other scientists called general relativity crazy, nonsense and a joke.

Some of these scientists were crackpots, but others were eminent scientists who were unable to understand Einstein's work. They still held on to the idea of the ether, even though there was no proof for it whatsoever. Some newspaper reporters jumped on to the bandwagon. They published articles saying Einstein was a crank. Unfortunately, in Germany, the level of criticism was to get worse.

Einstein's personality

Einstein normally had a sunny disposition, and often cheered up the people he met and talked to. He had an explosive laugh and was rarely annoyed or angry. He was very modest about his genius, and he never boasted about it. He said: "I am neither very clever nor especially gifted. I am only very, very curious." He always said that his theories were just theories, and might not be true, and could never be proved right or wrong. He also acknowledged that much of his work was developed from other people's work, and was not all his own idea. His only ambition was to find answers to scientific problems. Einstein hated fuss, as well as the formality and official functions that his fame brought. He even went into hiding on his 50th birthday (in 1929) to avoid having to see well-wishers.

Einstein never felt that he was more important than other people, and he treated everyone he met in the same way, from fellow scientists to prime ministers to children next door. He also helped out people whenever he could. Sometimes it was simply helping local children with their homework. At other times it was helping refugees to escape from persecution in Europe before and during World War Two (1939–45).

At home, Einstein led a simple life. Of his few personal possessions, his violin and his pipe were most valuable to him. His office at home was full of books, papers and portraits of the great scientists. All the tools he needed for work, he said, were paper and a pencil.

Einstein preferred simple food and clothes. He didn't believe in buying new clothes when his old ones were serviceable, and he often wore things that didn't match. He was also well known for being absent-minded.

Sudden fame changes some people, but it didn't change Albert Einstein. He refused the large salaries offered by universities and only accepted expenses for his lectures. He always travelled third-class on the train and stayed in simple accommodation rather than luxurious hotels. He never learned to drive and preferred to walk to places when he could.

▶ *Einstein never desired the luxuries and privileges that came with celebrity but he did enjoy simple pleasures. Here he is photographed sailing with Elsa in 1928.*

Attacks and the Nobel Prize

World War One ended in November 1918. Germany had surrendered, and the Allied countries made harsh demands.

Germany had to give up some of its land to France and Poland, it was ordered to pay for the damage the war had caused and parts of Germany were occupied by Allied troops. Just before war ended there had been a revolution by workers and troops in Germany, who tried to stop the war. Emperor Wilhelm II fled the country, and in 1919 there were elections that created a democracy in Germany, called the Weimar Republic.

Many Germans, especially some army officers, were not happy with the new government. Defeat in the war had left Germany extremely poor. There were food shortages and unemployment was high. People protested in the streets of German cities. Many Germans said the Jews were responsible for their defeat and the social conditions. This was untrue and unfair. In fact, twelve thousand Jews had died fighting in the trenches for Germany. But the people wanted somebody to blame. The Jews were an easy target and this anti-Semitic prejudice quickly spread.

Einstein was a German Jew. In the 1920s some Germans denigrated his theory of general relativity simply because he was Jewish. They said the work of a Jew must be wrong. Einstein received verbal threats in the street and hate mail through the post. Jokes and cartoons about him appeared in the papers. One top German scientist, Philipp Lenard, had praised Einstein in the past, but now he formed a group of anti-Semitic scientists that became known as the Anti-Relativity League. Einstein, with the support of his friends, tried to talk to

▶ *Einstein travels through New York in an open-top vehicle in 1921, and is greeted by crowds of well-wishers. He made many lecture tours to raise funds for a Jewish state.*

Anti-Semitism and Zionism

Anti-Semitism is prejudice against Jews. For hundreds of years, small groups of Jews in different countries were often unfairly blamed for social and economic problems. Some countries deported Jews, others forced them to live in ghettoes. Because of this, in the 1800s Jews began a movement called Zionism. Zionists campaigned for the formation of a Jewish homeland in Palestine, where Jews could escape from anti-Semitism and live safely. In 1948, the State of Israel, where many Jews now live, was created in Palestine.

them about his ideas, but they simply insulted him.

In 1922, Walter Rathenau, the Jewish foreign minister of Germany and a friend of Einstein, was shot dead in his car. Einstein learned that anti-Semites were offering a reward for his own death. Although Einstein was nervous about the situation, and friends offered him work outside Germany, he refused to leave Berlin because he wanted to keep working with his fellow scientists at the university.

Einstein supports Zionism

In 1921 the Zionist leader Chaim Weizmann (1874–1952) persuaded Einstein to go on a lecture tour of the United States to help to raise funds for the Palestine Foundation Fund. At first Einstein was reluctant, but he was soon persuaded, perhaps because of the anti-Semitism he was witnessing in Berlin. In New York, Albert and Elsa were greeted like royalty. Einstein was amazed by the city's huge buildings, bright lights and the gadgets in people's homes. The couple made a whirlwind tour of the USA, visiting Chicago, Washington and Boston. In Chicago, Einstein met Robert Millikan, the scientist who had proved the existence of the photoelectric effect, and Albert Michelson, the man who had failed to find the ether. On his way home Einstein stopped off in London, England, and laid flowers on Isaac Newton's grave.

Lecture tours

After the solar eclipse of 1919, honours and awards from scientific bodies were heaped on Einstein. Everybody wanted a piece of him. There were invitations from countries all over the world for him to visit and lecture about his theories. The

▼ A photograph taken at a station in Palestine on the return journey from Japan, February 1923. Albert and Elsa Einstein are shown with the mayor of Tel Aviv, Meir Dizengoff and the Zionists Bezalel Jaffe and Benzion Mossinson.

media followed him wherever he went. People were fascinated by him, and his lectures were enormously popular and tickets always sold out. He spoke slowly and softly, and tried to explain his difficult theories as simply as possible so that everybody could understand them.

During the 1920s, Einstein travelled by train and ship, always with his violin, to all parts of Europe, to the United States, to Asia, to the Middle East and South America. He met heads of state, royalty, top scientists and everyday people. He especially loved Japan. Here, thousands of people stood in the street outside his hotel all night to catch a glimpse of him. Tours and visits like these would continue until Einstein was forced to move to the USA in the early 1930s.

Whenever he was back in Berlin, there were sacks of letters to reply to, asking all kinds of questions on all sorts of subjects. In addition, there were constant phone calls, and a continuous stream of visitors wanting to talk to him and interview him. Elsa and Margot made sure that only some of these requests got through to

A photograph of Einstein taken in 1925, the year before he completed his first version of the controversial unified field theory.

Einstein. He normally crept out of the house by the back door if he did not want to be found.

A Nobel Prize at last

Einstein was first nominated for the Nobel Prize for physics in 1909, for his theory of special relativity. He had been nominated nearly every year between then and 1921, when he finally won. He had to wait all this time because of the judges' inability to understand the importance of relativity, and possibly also because of anti-Semitism. And even when the prize was finally awarded to him it was not for his theory of relativity. His Nobel Prize was awarded for "services to theoretical physics, and especially for the discovery of the law of the photoelectric effect". Einstein was in Shanghai, in China,

Nobel Prizes

Nobel Prizes are awarded to people or organizations who have made the greatest contribution in their particular field. There are prizes for physics, chemistry, medicine, literature, economics and world peace. They are named after the Swedish chemist Alfred Nobel (1833–1896), the inventor of dynamite, who left the prize fund in his will.

Einstein meets Freud

Einstein's world fame meant that he was introduced to many of the great public figures of the time. Among these figures was Sigmund Freud (1856–1939), above. Freud was an Austrian doctor who studied psychiatry and psychology, and developed the theory of psychoanalysis, which made him as famous as Einstein himself. Freud and Einstein met for the first time in 1926 in Berlin, when Freud was 70 years old. Einstein joked that he avoided being analyzed by Freud. The two men exchanged many letters about pacifism and politics. In one of these, Einstein commented that because of the never-ending round of wars across the world, humans must enjoy hating and destroying each other. Freud agreed. Like Einstein, Freud was a Jew, and he left Austria for England after the Nazis invaded in 1938.

▶ *Einstein gives a lecture at the College de France, in Paris, in 1921. The audience listens intently.*

when he received the news by telegram. He didn't actually go to Sweden to collect his Nobel medal until 1923. True to form, he made his acceptance speech in an old crumpled jacket, and sent the $32,500 prize money to Mileva, as he had promised to do five years before.

The unified field theory

Einstein's next major project was to try to find a link between the two forces of electromagnetism and gravity. Most scientists thought they were completely separate from each other, but Einstein suspected that they might be different forms of the same thing. He tried to find mathematical equations that would show this link. This was the first stage in what he called his unified field theory. His long-term aim was to develop a theory that explained every force in the universe, and so describe how everything in the universe works, from the tiny particles in atoms to the stars and planets. Einstein spent most of the 1920s working on it. In 1928, months of enforced rest after an illness allowed him to think about his theory without interruption,

and he published the first version of his new theory in 1929. The media were gripped by the great scientist's latest thoughts, but his fellow scientists were less impressed. They knew that the published work was only a starting point, and thought that Einstein's theories were heading in completely the wrong direction. Einstein himself realized there was a great deal of hard work to be done before unified field theory would be completed, so he didn't worry about criticism from other scientists too much. However, in the end, he would spend the rest of his life working on the unified field theory, without ever finding an answer. The problem was extremely complicated, and there were many unknown factors to take into account. He remarked that it might be better if he could prove that the problem was impossible to solve, so that he could stop trying to find the solution. Eventually, late in life, Einstein would admit defeat.

◀ *Albert Einstein delivered a series of lectures on his theory of relativity at Oxford University. This photograph was taken at the university on 23 May 1931, the day that the honorary degree of Doctor of Science was conferred on him.*

Threats and warnings

Throughout the late 1920s and early 1930s, Einstein lived in Berlin, lectured at Berlin University, travelled to many different countries and continued to develop his unified field theory.

Most of his fellow theoretical physicists did not believe that Einstein's unified field theory would be the answer to how the universe works. They thought he was going down a blind alley, and they told him so. Some scientists, like Niels Bohr (1885–1962), were disappointed by his stubbornness. They felt that the efforts Einstein was putting into the unified field theory could be better put to use helping them with their new quantum theory.

Quantum theory attempts to explain what happens inside atoms and how atoms give off and absorb light and other forms of radiation. The idea was started by Max Planck with his thought that electromagnetic waves come in little

▶ *A photograph of Einstein's summer house at Caputh bei Potsdam. He lived here from 1929–32, but had to spend much of his time away travelling.*

packets of energy, which he called quanta. Einstein himself carried on the ideas with his theory that light is made up of packets of energy, called photons. In 1913, Niels Bohr used quantum theory to explain how atoms give off light. In 1927, Werner Heisenberg (1901–1976) took the theory further. He introduced what is called the uncertainty principle. This stated that mathematics can only predict where a sub-atomic particle probably is, and not exactly where it is.

Predicting particle activity

Einstein agreed with some aspects of quantum theory, and he tried to include them in his unified field theory. But he never agreed with the uncertainty principle. He said it should always be possible to predict what a particle was going to do next. "God does not play dice with the world," he said. He had many heated discussions with Bohr about quantum theory. He joked that scientists had introduced probability into the theory simply because they could not

▶ *The "Party Day of the Victorious" in Nuremberg, Germany, which took place between 1–3 September in 1933. This rally of Hitler Youth and many other young people was held in the Nuremberg Stadium. Up to 80,000 people participated.*

The rise of the Nazis

While Einstein was working in Berlin, the National Socialist German Workers Party, or the Nazi Party, was steadily gaining strength in Germany. The party was founded in 1919, and Adolf Hitler became its leader the same year. The Nazis attempted to take power by force in 1923, but failed. Despite this setback, Hitler was still campaigning in 1925 and he told his followers that the Jews were partly to blame for Germany's terrible economic and social problems. As a result, anti-Semitism grew stronger and Hitler's popularity increased. In 1929 there was a world-wide economic depression. Millions of Germans lost their jobs, and there were fuel and food shortages. The Nazis took advantage of the nation's distress. They promised to make Germany powerful again, and so restore prosperity.

In 1933 the Nazis finally came to power. Hitler was appointed German chancellor, but soon made himself dictator. One of his aims was to rid Germany of all people who he thought were inferior to "real" Germans, and this included the Jews. Laws to persecute and isolate the Jews were created. For example, Jewish lecturers were thrown out of their jobs and the Gestapo (secret police) closed Jewish shops. Later in the 1930s Jews who had not already fled Germany were rounded up and put into concentration camps, where millions would die during World War Two, in what is now known as the Holocaust.

work out what was going on. In 1930, he said, "If quantum physics is right, the world is crazy!"

Einstein and pacifism

After World War One, Einstein wanted a world government to be set up to prevent another such appalling war. He became a member of the German Peace Federation. In 1920, an international organization called the League of Nations was created to try to maintain world peace. Along with other top scientists and thinkers worldwide, Einstein was elected to the League's Committee on Intellectual Co-operation. By 1930, he realized that the League of Nations had little power to stop countries fighting, and so he resigned.

In 1932 Einstein established the Einstein War Resisters' International Fund. This fund was designed to help persuade governments to disarm their armies. But international disarmament talks were a failure, leaving Einstein disappointed and angry.

Einstein was also dismayed at the widespread support for the Nazis, as well

◀ Einstein on the journey from New York to Antwerp in March 1933, about the time he was told that the Nazis had stolen his property and taken away his job.

as the rising tide of anti-Semitism in Germany. He had thought that defeat in World War One had put an end to German militarism, but now it looked as though Germany was building up for another war. He perceived the Nazis as a serious threat to world peace and so his pacifist ideals began to shift. He did not want to see another war, but believed that other countries must defend themselves against German aggression.

Trips to the USA

In December 1930, Einstein went to the USA for two months to visit Caltech (California Institute of Technology) and the Mount Wilson Observatory. He hoped that the visit would help him resolve some of the problems he was having with his unified field theory. He met top American cosmologists, including Edwin Hubble (1889–1953). Hubble had just discovered that distant galaxies appear to be moving away from our own, showing that the universe is expanding. On one visit to the Mount Wilson Observatory, Einstein heard a scientist say that he thought the universe had started with a giant explosion. Einstein was heard to say "This is the most beautiful and satisfactory explanation of creation to which I have ever listened." It was not all work, however. With Elsa, he visited some Hollywood film studios and met Charlie Chaplin, the biggest star of silent films.

Late in 1931, Einstein returned to Caltech for several months. On this trip he met Abraham Flexner, an educator. Flexner told Einstein of his idea to set up an establishment in the USA where elite scientists from around the world could work together. The establishment would be called the Institute for Advanced Study, based at Princeton, New Jersey. He invited Einstein to join. After refusing once, Einstein accepted. However, he wanted to return to Berlin for six months every year, and bring his assistant, Walther Mayer, with him to Princeton.

A voyage of no return

Einstein left Berlin for another stint at Caltech in December 1932. He had already suffered from anti-Semitism in Germany and knew that with the stranglehold the Nazis had on power, things could only get worse. Einstein suspected that, sadly, this time it might be impossible for him to return home. His

suspicions proved to be right. On his return to Europe, he found out that the Nazis had ransacked his home and confiscated his property, including his boat. They had also taken away his job at Berlin University, and declared that he was an enemy of Germany. Now he knew he could never go home.

Elsa's daughters and Einstein's secretary, Helen Dukas, joined him in Belgium. When Einstein was told that there was a reward of $5,000 on his head, he simply said, "I didn't know I was worth that much!" They were all protected by armed guards. He visited England, where he met Winston Churchill, a Member of Parliament who was to become Britain's wartime leader. He warned Churchill that Germany was getting ready for a war.

In autumn 1933 the Einsteins went to Princeton for Einstein to take up his job. He didn't realize then that he would spend the rest of his life there, never to return to Germany. Over the next few years, Einstein would help many other Jewish friends flee Nazi Germany.

▶ *Einstein and Member of Parliament Oliver Locker-Lampson at his country house in Roughton Heath, Cromer, Norfolk, in September 1933. Einstein stayed at the country house for a month.*

Life in the USA

Einstein settled down to a new life in Princeton. In 1935, he bought a small, simple house about two kilometres from the new Institute for Advanced Study in Princeton.

He lived there with Elsa, her daughter Margot and his secretary Helen Dukas. Every day, he walked to the Institute, refusing the regular offers of lifts. At home he worked alone in his untidy study. As always, he played his violin and sailed a boat. Einstein loved the peace and quiet of sailing. He would often sit becalmed on the lake rather than use the engine.

People thought Einstein was an expert on everything. His mail was full of questions on every possible subject. There were also occasional marriage proposals. Anything he said publicly about science and politics appeared in the press. Elsa,

▶ *Albert Einstein and Elsa's daughter Margot (standing at Einstein's left-hand side) pledge allegiance as they take US citizenship in 1940.*

Helen Dukas and helpful neighbours dealt with the avalanche of letters, and kept the visitors and the press at bay. Einstein spent weekends and holidays with his many friends and neighbours. There were always people willing to do him favours and drive him from place to place. He also found time to play games with local children and help them with their homework.

In 1936, Elsa died of heart and liver disease. Einstein's sister Maja left Germany for the USA and lived near him in Princeton. She had a stroke in 1946 and while she was ill, Einstein visited her every day. She died in 1951. Back in 1933, Einstein, Margot and Helen Dukas had renounced their German citizenship. In 1940 Einstein became a US citizen.

Einstein was always interested in human affairs, and he constantly tried to help political or social victims. While in Berlin he raised money for refugees moving into the city, and he helped people to escape from persecution in Nazi Germany. He even auctioned his own valuable books to raise funds to help refugees. Unfortunately, there were anti-Semites in the USA as well as Germany, and Einstein continued to get hate mail from Nazi supporters living there. He never returned to Germany because he was so appalled at the way his fellow Germans had treated the Jews. Like millions of Jews, Einstein lost several relatives in the Holocaust. He also spoke out against the discrimination against black citizens that was taking place in some southern US states.

Bomb warnings

In 1938 experiments carried out in Germany by scientist Otto Hahn (1879–1968) showed that it was possible to split an atom. This nuclear reaction would release massive amounts of energy, as predicted by Einstein's famous equation $E = mc^2$. Niels Bohr relayed the news to Einstein in the USA. Bohr explained that it could be possible to make an atomic bomb if the reaction in one atom could be used to set off other reactions, creating a chain reaction. Einstein knew this was possible in theory, but he doubted that it would be possible to make it work. However, he grew worried. In 1939, Einstein signed a letter, written by other concerned scientists, to President Roosevelt. The letter warned Roosevelt that it could be possible to make a bomb with a terrifyingly destructive force. It explained that the Nazis were probably already working on the idea, and if they successfully built such a bomb, they would probably use it.

The US government reacted slowly, but eventually started work. They set up what was called the Manhattan Project in order to develop an atomic bomb. It was Einstein's work that had predicted how much energy could be released by a bomb, but he himself was not invited to help on the project. In fact, like most Americans, he knew nothing about it because it was top secret. However, when Einstein heard about the atrocities against Jews and others in Europe and Asia, he volunteered to work on weapons research that was less secret for the navy, and helped to design automatic torpedoes.

Peace proposals

Einstein only found out that the USA had successfully built an atomic bomb at the same time as the rest of the world. It was on 6 August 1945, when an atomic bomb was dropped on Hiroshima, Japan, destroying the city in seconds, and killing 200,000 people. Einstein was horrified by the destructive power of the bomb. Possibly he felt in some way responsible for the atomic bomb because he was the physicist who had revealed the enormous energy contained in matter. "Alas, oh my God!" he said. "If I knew they were going to do this, I would have become a shoemaker!"

The threat of nuclear war

Einstein knew that other countries would eventually develop and build their own nuclear bombs. He feared that there was a high chance of a nuclear war that would almost destroy the world. He wrote to President Truman asking for an international ban on nuclear weapons.

Through letters to the international press, he pleaded for governments of all countries to come together for world peace. In 1946, along with other top physicists, he formed a group called the Emergency Committee of Atomic Scientists, which tried to publicize the threat of a nuclear war. Many people believed that his desire for a world government was unrealistic. Einstein himself knew it would be almost impossible to achieve. "Politics is harder than physics," he admitted.

A photograph of the destroyed city of Hiroshima on 6 August 1945 provides terrifying evidence of the damage and devastation caused by one atomic bomb.

Support of Zionism

Einstein's support for Zionism grew as he witnessed the suffering of Jews before and during World War Two. After the war the British were left in charge of Palestine, where Zionists wanted the new Jewish homeland to be. However, there were far more Arabs living there than Jews. Einstein said that the Jews needed a safe home, but he was concerned for the Arabs, too. He said they should not suffer in order to create a separate country for Jews. He argued that Arabs and Jews should share Palestine, run by an international government.

The Cold War

In the 1950s and 1960s the USA and the Soviet Union had different, opposing political systems. There was communism in the Soviet Union and capitalism in the USA. This caused deep mistrust between the two sides. Each thought the other wanted to dominate the world, and they built huge numbers of nuclear weapons. This period was known as the Cold War.

However, in 1947, the United Nations voted that Palestine should be divided between the Arabs and the Jews. The State of Israel came into being in 1948, as Arabs and Jews fought over Palestine. After the first president of Israel died in 1952, the Israelis invited Einstein to become their next president. He turned them down, saying that he regretted having to do so, but that he felt unsuited to the job because he was not good at dealing with people.

Fading powers

Einstein continued to try to find the answer to the riddles of the universe. He carried on working on relativity and his unified field theory. In 1950, he published a new version of the unified field theory, but he was criticized again. Einstein's work was now largely ignored by mainstream theoretical physicists. Some were quite rude about him. For example, Robert Oppenheimer, who led the USA's atomic bomb project, said Einstein was "completely cuckoo". In 1951, Einstein accepted that he would never complete

◀ *Einstein pictured in his study at Princeton in 1949, surrounded by books and papers.*

his unified field theory. He said somebody else would have to do it instead.

As he got older, Einstein felt that his powers of thought were disappearing. It was not that he couldn't think about a

The FBI investigates

During the Cold War of the 1950s, suspected communists were being hunted in the USA. The Federal Bureau of Investigation (FBI) suspected that Einstein was a communist sympathizer, and possibly a spy for the Soviet Union.

They were suspicious of Einstein for several reasons. He supported peace movements and oppressed people. He said that the Soviet Union was not entirely to blame for the Cold War and expressed concern that the USA might be heading the same way as Germany in the 1920s, so people might be better off in the Soviet Union. He also supported the Jewish husband and wife Julius and Ethel Rosenberg, who were sentenced to death for passing atomic secrets to the Soviets. He supported them not because of their links to the Soviets, but because he thought the evidence against them was weak.

The FBI investigated Einstein's affairs for nine years, without him ever knowing. They never found any evidence against him. Along with Einstein, they also investigated his secretary Helen Dukas.

particular problem, but that he could not decide what problem to choose to work on. He said that new discoveries were made by younger minds, and was a little depressed that some of the owners of these younger minds thought he was an eccentric old fool. Einstein never wrote an autobiography, although he was offered plenty of money to do so. However, he did write a book about his work, called *Autobiographical Notes*.

Illness and death

After collapsing in 1928, Einstein had been diagnosed with heart trouble. At the time he had spent a year on sick leave from Berlin University, but he kept on working at home. He also became a vegetarian to reduce the effects of liver disease. More heart problems surfaced in 1948, which eventually stopped him from sailing and smoking his pipe. On 18 April 1955, Albert Einstein died in his sleep in Princeton Hospital, after having been housebound for several months. He was 76 years old. After his body was cremated, his ashes were scattered on the Delaware River.

▶ *Albert Einstein photographed in Princeton in 1938, the year before World War Two began.*

Einstein's legacy

Today, Albert Einstein's legacy continues, and he remains a towering figure in the world of science. His ideas and theories, especially special and general relativity, have exerted a huge influence in the fields of particle physics and cosmology.

Scientists have found new evidence that supports Einstein's theories, continued to develop his ideas and used them to predict the behaviour of sub-atomic particles and the existence of bizarre objects in space, such as black holes and wormholes. We see the practical applications of his famous equation $E=mc^2$ in areas as diverse as nuclear power stations, medical scanners and smoke alarms.

Evidence for relativity

Since Einstein's death, plenty of evidence has been found to support his theory of relativity. In 1979 astronomers found a double image of a quasar. A quasar looks like a star, but gives out billions of times more energy. The double image was caused because light from the quasar was bent round either side of a massive object deep in space. This effect is called a gravitational lens because the distortion of space and time bends the light the same way a lens does. In the 1990s, photographs taken by the Hubble Space Telescope showed galaxies that looked distorted because light from them was bent as it travelled to Earth. It was like looking through an old glass window.

Gravity waves

Einstein's theory of general relativity predicted that if a mass changes speed or direction, then it sends out waves like ripples spreading on a pond. But these waves distort space and time as they pass. They are called gravity waves. Some evidence for gravity waves has been seen

▶ This Hubble Space Telescope image of the so-called "Einstein's Cross" is an example of gravitational lensing. The central spot is a relatively nearby galaxy, while the four outer spots are images of a distant quasar. Light from the quasar has been bent by the gravitational field of the intervening galaxy, which acts as a giant lens, and forms four images of the quasar. Einstein predicted this effect in 1926.

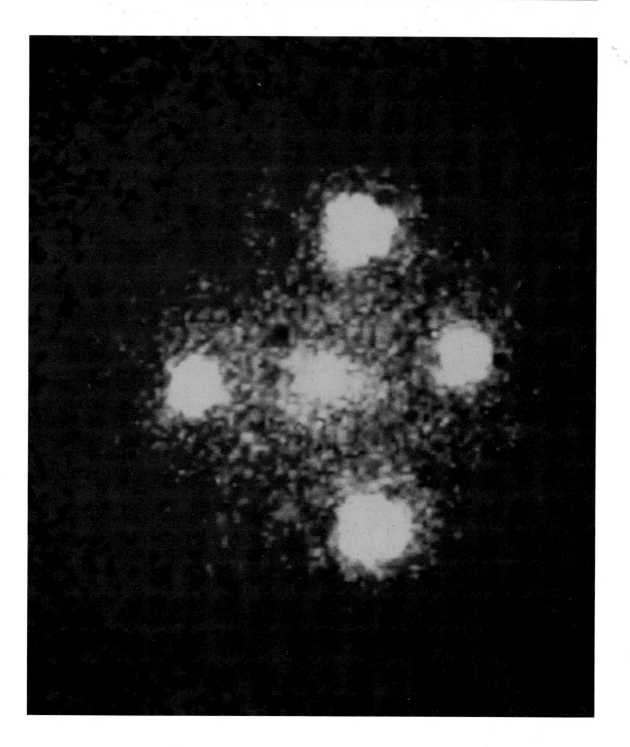

in the movement of objects in deep space. But so far, nobody has detected a gravity wave because gravity waves from even the most enormous masses are incredibly weak. But the search for them is on, because gravity waves would tell us about the movements of invisible matter in space, nicknamed "dark matter". NASA is due to launch a spacecraft in 2006 to detect gravity waves.

Black holes and wormholes

A black hole is an object in space that is very small but incredibly heavy. Black holes are created when enormous stars die and collapse in on themselves. It is thought that the concentrated mass of a black hole distorts space and time so much that not even light can escape from it. Because no light can escape, we can't see black holes, but we can detect gas from nearby stars being pulled into them. If you ever fell into a black hole, your body would probably be pulled to pieces by the distorted space inside.

Einstein's theory of general relativity shows that because space and time can be distorted, a straight line is not necessarily the shortest route from one place to another. This has led some scientists to predict that huge amounts of energy could be used to create space-time short-cuts, called wormholes.

The expanding universe and the Big Bang

Isaac Newton thought the universe was infinitely big and that the stars were static (that is, not moving in relation to each other). His ideas were accepted for more than a hundred years. Then in 1826 a scientist called Heinrich Olber realized that if the universe was infinitely big, light from the infinite number of stars in it would make the night sky look white. So he thought it must be finite, and if so, it must be expanding. Otherwise it would collapse under its own gravity.

Einstein also thought the universe was finite, but that it was static. However, he realized that his theory of general relativity predicted that the universe should be expanding. He thought that some undiscovered force between objects must be responsible for keeping

▶ *An artificially-coloured bubble-chamber photo taken at CERN, the European particle physics laboratory outside Geneva, shows the breathtaking symmetry of tracks made by split atoms.*

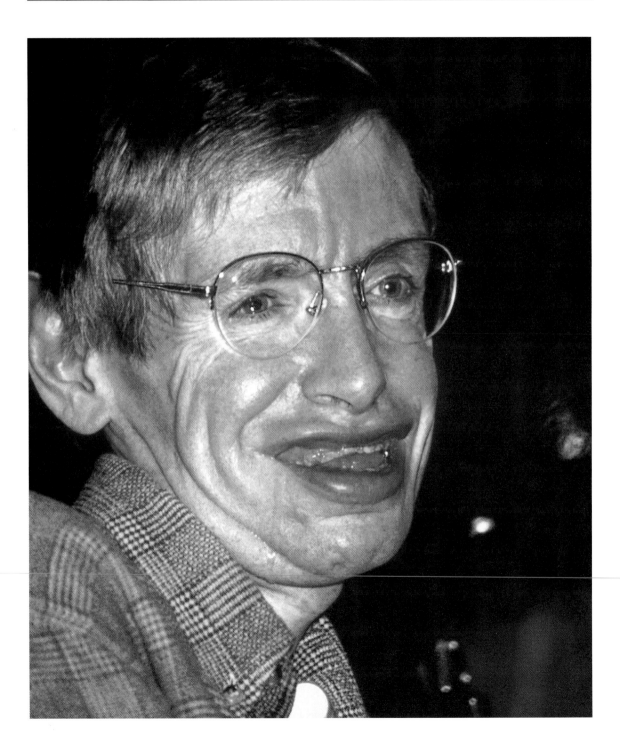

it static, and so introduced a new force into his theory.

In 1929 Edwin Hubble discovered that all the galaxies in the universe are moving away from each other, and the farther away they are, the faster they are moving away. This was proof that showed that the universe is expanding. Other cosmologists used relativity to show that an expanding universe was possible without Einstein's new force. Einstein admitted he had made "the biggest blunder of my life".

The expanding universe idea led to the Big Bang theory. If the universe is expanding, it must have started expanding from somewhere. By measuring the speeds of galaxies and working backwards, cosmologists have concluded that the universe must have started expanding with an unimaginably enormous explosion between 10,000 and 20,000 million years ago. This was the Big Bang. They think that a tiny fraction of a second after the Big Bang began, all

◀ *Today Stephen Hawking, the English theoretical physicist, carries on examining general relativity and is well known for his work on black holes, Big Bang theory and gravitational field theory. Despite suffering from motor neurone disease he has also written a best-selling book, **A Brief History of Time**.*

Crunch or yawn?

What does relativity predict will happen to the universe in the future? Scientists say it all depends on how much hidden "dark" matter is out in space. The universe could eventually stop expanding and collapse again. The result would be the opposite of the Big Bang, which cosmologists have nicknamed the Big Crunch.

This could be followed by a new Big Bang. On the other hand, the universe could carry on expanding for ever. This scenario is known as the Big Yawn.

the matter in the universe was in the form of energy, in a space smaller than a garden pea. Nobody knows what happened before the Big Bang.

New theories

Theoretical physicists such as Stephen Hawking (b. 1942) continue to develop relativity and quantum theory, and are trying to produce an overall theory to explain matter and the universe. Half a century after Einstein was criticized for his attempts to find a unified field theory, physicists are once again trying to link electromagnetic radiation and gravity.

We still have far more to find out about the universe than we already know, but it's likely that we would never even have got this far without the ingenious work of Albert Einstein. He changed our understanding of matter and the universe for ever. For this reason, he has been called the greatest scientist since Isaac Newton.

Einstein is far less famous for his work in the areas of peace and humanity, perhaps because they were less successful than his work in science. But he probably knew that this would happen. "Politics are for the moment," he said. "An equation is for eternity."

Einstein's brain

After Einstein died, a pathologist called Thomas Harvey performed an autopsy to find the cause of death. During the autopsy, he removed Einstein's brain. Amazingly, he kept the brain in a jar in the basement of his house. He sent some sections of the brain for analysis in case it could be worked out why Einstein was so intelligent. Scientists who have studied sections say that it looks like the brain of a much younger person. As far as we know, Thomas Harvey still has the rest of it.

▶ *A formal portrait photograph of Albert Einstein dating from the 1930s.*

Glossary

acceleration A change in the velocity (either the speed or direction) of an object.

anti-Semitism Prejudice against Jews.

arc light A type of light that creates intense light. It works by allowing electricity to jump across a gap, in effect creating a continuous spark.

atom The basic building block of all matter. Atoms are the smallest particles of matter that exist.

Brownian motion The random motion of microscopic particles in a liquid, caused by the liquid's molecules bumping into them.

cosmology The study of the whole universe and how it was formed.

disarmament Taking away or giving up weapons of war.

dynamo A device similar to an electric motor, but which does the opposite job to a motor. It produces electricity when its spindle is turned.

electromagnetic radiation An alternative name for any electromagnetic wave.

electromagnetic wave A wave made up of electric and magnetic waves that can travel through a vacuum. Light, radio waves and microwaves are examples of electromagnetic waves.

electron One of the particles that makes up an atom.

energy The ability to make things happen. Nothing can happen without it.

ether An imaginary substance that was once thought to fill the whole of space, allowing light to travel.

gravity A force that attracts two objects together. Gravity between you and the Earth gives you your weight.

Judaism The religion of the Jewish people.

mass A measure of the resistance of an object to change its movement, which is also a measure of the amount of matter in the object.

molecule The smallest particle of a substance. Most molecules are made up of two or more atoms joined together.

Nazi A member of the Nazi (National Socialist) Party that ruled Germany in the 1930s and 1940s.

observer A person who is watching an event.

orbit The path that a planet follows around the Sun.

photoelectric effect This effect occurs when light hitting the surface of a metal knocks out electrons, allowing an electric current to flow.

radioactivity Streams of particles and electromagnetic waves, together called radiation, given off by radioactive substances.

solar eclipse An event that happens when the Moon passes between the Earth and the Sun, casting its shadow on the Earth's surface.

sub-atomic particle Any particle that makes up an atom.

theory of general relativity Einstein's theory, published in 1916, that links together movement, light, space and time.

theory of special relativity Einstein's theory, published in 1905, that links together space, time and gravity.

vacuum A place where there is nothing.

velocity The speed and direction of an object.

Zionism A political movement that campaigned for the formation of a homeland for all Jews.

Timeline

1879 14 March Albert Einstein is born in Ulm, Germany.

1881 The Einstein family moves to Munich to set up business.

1888 Einstein begins elementary school.

1894 Einstein drops out of high school to follow his family to Milan.

1895 Einstein goes to school in Switzerland to complete his high-school certificate.

1897 Einstein begins studying physics at the Federal Institute of Technology, Zürich.

1901 Einstein becomes a Swiss citizen.

1902 Einstein begins work at the Swiss patent office, Bern.

1902 Einstein's father Hermann dies.

1903 Einstein is married to Mileva Maric, a fellow student at the Federal Institute of Technology.

1904 The Einsteins' first son, Hans Albert, is born.

1905 Four of Einstein's scientific papers are published, including his explanations of the photoelectric effect and Brownian motion, and his theory of special relativity.

1909 Einstein resigns from the Swiss patent office to become professor of physics at Zürich University.

1910 The Einsteins' second son, Eduard, is born.

1911 Einstein moves to the German University in Prague.

1912 Einstein moves to the Federal Institute of Technology, Zürich.

1913 Einstein moves to Berlin to work at Berlin University.

1914 World War One begins.

1914 Einstein's marriage to Mileva Maric breaks down.

1916 Einstein publishes his theory of general relativity.

1918 World War One ends.

1919 Einstein and Mileva Maric are divorced, and later the same year Einstein marries Elsa Löwenthall.

1919 The theory of general relativity is proved during a solar eclipse.

1920 Einstein's mother Pauline dies.

1921 Einstein is awarded the Nobel Prize for physics.

1921 Einstein goes on a lecture tour of the USA to raise money for Zionism.

1926 The first version of Einstein's controversial unified field theory is completed.

1930 Einstein visits the California Institute of Technology for the first time.

1933 The Nazis gain power in Germany.

1933 Einstein begins work at the Institute for Advanced Study, Princeton, USA.

1939 World War Two begins, and Einstein warns the US authorities of the possibility of a German nuclear bomb.

1940 Einstein becomes a US citizen.

1945 The first atomic bomb is dropped on Hiroshima, Japan, and World War Two comes to an end.

1952 Einstein turns down an offer to become president of Israel.

1955 18 April Einstein dies.

Further reading

Einstein – A Beginner's Guide
Jim Breithaupt
Hodder and Stoughton 2000

Einstein – A Life in Science
John Gribbin & Michael White
Pocket Books 1997

Einstein – A Life
Denis Brian
John Wiley & Sons 1996

$E=mc^2$
David Bodanis
Pan Books 2001

Introducing Einstein
Joseph Schwartz and Michael McGuiness
Icon Books 1999

Index

Page numbers in italics are pictures or maps.